Canadian Families

CANADIAN FUN AND GAMES

TRUE NORTH

BY PAULA MORROW

True North is published by Beech Street Books
27 Stewart Rd. Collingwood, ON Canada L9Y 4M7

www.beechstreetbooks.ca

Produced by Red Line Editorial

Photographs ©: O'SHI/Shutterstock Images, cover, 1; Jeffrey B. Banke/Shutterstock Images, 4–5; Ccyyrree, 6; Serkan Senturk/ Shutterstock Images, 8–9; EPA European Pressphoto Agency B.V./Alamy, 10–11; Roman Babakin/Shutterstock Images, 12; James A. Boardman/Shutterstock Images, 14–15; Red Line Editorial, 16; Ethan Daniels/Shutterstock Images, 18–19; Pierre Leclerc/Shutterstock Images, 20

Editor: Heather C. Hudak
Designer: Laura Polzin

Library and Archives Canada Cataloguing in Publication

 Morrow, Paula, author
        Canadian fun and games / by Paula Morrow.

(Canadian families)
Includes bibliographical references and index.
Issued in print and electronic formats.
ISBN 978-1-77308-008-6 (hardback).--ISBN 978-1-77308-036-9 (paperback).--ISBN 978-1-77308-064-2 (pdf).--ISBN 978-1-77308-092-5 (html)

        1. Amusements--Canada--Juvenile literature. 2. Games--Canada--Juvenile literature. 3. Family recreation--Canada--Juvenile literature. I. Title.

GV1204.15.M67 2016   j790.1'910971   C2016-903160-8
                                                   C2016-903161-6

Printed in the United States of America
Mankato, MN
August 2016

TABLE OF CONTENTS

Chapter One

MANY FESTIVALS

We are all Canadians, but we are not all alike. We have many cultures and **traditions**. Playing and having fun help us get to know each other. Festivals take place across the country. People use them to celebrate their history, cultures, and environments. Festivals are a great way to share our roots.

In 1896 gold was found in Yukon. Thousands of people rushed to the area to pan for gold. Today, people remember this time by holding the Yukon Gold **Panning** Championships. Tiny gold flakes are hidden in buckets of dirt.

Panners of all ages race to find gold in their buckets in Yukon.

People carve snow sculptures on the street for *Festival du Voyageur*.

6

In Yellowknife, Northwest Territories, the Caribou Carnival began as a gathering of fur trappers at the end of trapping season. Over time it has turned into a celebration of spring. Now people come for the dancing and fireworks. There is snow bowling, snow tennis, and ice **sculpting**.

Winter brings months of darkness high in the Arctic Circle. In January the Iglulingmiut people hold the Festival of the Return of the Sun. For five days they celebrate the end of winter darkness.

The *Festival du Voyageur* in Winnipeg, Manitoba, offers a taste of French tradition. It features singing, snow sculpting, and crafts. Folklorama is one of the biggest **multicultural** festivals in the world. Dozens of cultures host events. They dress in traditional clothing. They also put on dance shows and share their foods.

FAST FACT

In Alberta people come to Edmonton for the Servus Heritage Festival. More than 80 cultures share their foods, crafts, and artwork. The Calgary Stampede is more than 100 years old. It started as a rodeo for working cowboys to show off their skills. Today the rodeo is a way to remember Calgary's frontier days.

Out west the Kamloopa Powwow is one of Canada's largest First Nations festivals. Each year in August the Secwepemc Nation gathers in Kamloops, British Columbia. The celebration includes traditional storytelling, music, and dancing.

In Quebec Canada's French heritage is celebrated at the Quebec Winter Carnival. It features a moving snowman called Bonhomme Carnaval. His job is to represent French Quebec to visitors from all around the world. Quebec also has a big festival called *Festival d'eté de Québec* in July.

Canada's east coast has many festivals celebrating its unique culture. The Royal Nova Scotia International **Tattoo** is one of them. It is a huge gathering. Bagpipers, highland dancers, and military bands offer a taste of Scottish tradition. The March Hare started in Newfoundland and Labrador. It is an international poetry celebration. It **showcases** talented Canadian writers.

Bonhomme is a hit at the Quebec Winter Carnival.

Chapter Two

FALL AND WINTER FUN

Canadians take part in many outdoor sports and games during the winter. Some have been enjoyed since the country first formed. Others are much newer.

Thousands of years ago, Canada's Aboriginal Peoples began using snowshoes. Much later French traders held snowshoe races. Today many people enjoy snowshoeing across prairies and through forests.

Cross-country ski trails stretch all the way across Canada. You can ski from British Columbia to Nova Scotia. Trails also go north into Yukon and Newfoundland and Labrador.

Vancouver hosted the 2010 Winter Olympics. Many skiing events took place in the town of Whistler.

vancouver 2010

FAST FACT

Adult athletes come from all the provinces and territories to compete in the Canada Games. It switches between winter and summer every two years. Children from kindergarten to grade eight participate in Canada Games Days. They are held at schools all across Canada.

Snowmobile trails stretch from Newfoundland and Labrador all the way to western Vancouver, British Columbia.

Downhill skiing sends people speeding down steep slopes. The Canadian Rocky Mountains are home to many great ski slopes. Other top-level slopes are Mont-Tremblant in Quebec and Blue Mountain in Ontario.

The Iroquois crossed frozen lakes using animal shin bones as skates. British soldiers had ice-skating races. Every province has many skating rinks. People skate on lakes and rivers, too.

The longest skating track is 10 kilometres long. It is at Sylvan Lake, Alberta.

Aboriginal Peoples used toboggans to carry supplies across the snow. Over time people began using toboggans for sledding. Today people use sleds to slide down hills in winter.

A snowmobile can travel long distances at fast speeds. The caterpillar **treads** can travel over snow, ice, and slush. The wet, heavy snow of southern Canada is especially good for snowmobiling.

Hockey is the national winter sport. European settlers brought the game to Canada. They played it on the ice with a stick and a ball. Canadians began playing hockey on ice in the 1800s. They used a flat wooden puck instead of a ball.

Ringette is a winter sport. It was invented in Canada in 1963. It is similar to hockey. It is played with a rubber ring instead of a puck.

Chapter Three

SPRING AND SUMMER GAMES

Sports are an important part of Canadian culture. Lacrosse is Canada's national summer sport. It grew from ball games played by the First Nations. The Iroquois were known for their skill in this sport.

The British brought soccer and rugby to Canada in the 1800s. Soccer is the number one team sport played by Canadian children. Football is a popular summer sport. Nine cities have teams in the Canadian Football League (CFL). Many people enjoy watching CFL games. Rugby is

Crosse was the name French settlers gave lacrosse. They may have thought the stick looked like a Bishop's crosier, or staff.

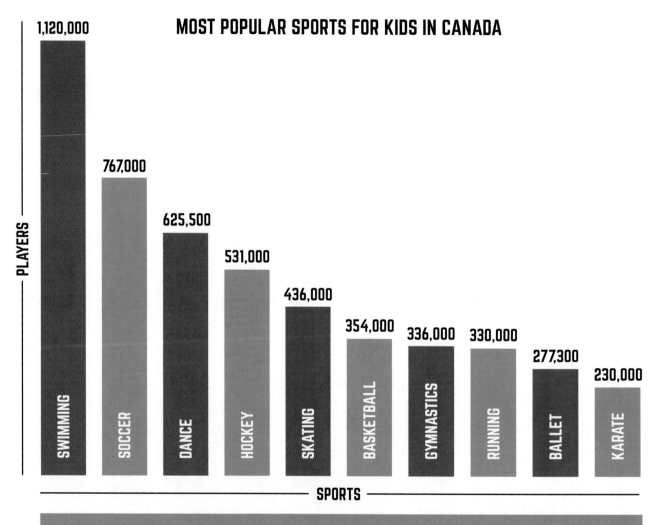

MOST POPULAR SPORTS FOR KIDS IN CANADA

PLAYERS

SPORTS

1,120,000	SWIMMING	
767,000	SOCCER	
625,500	DANCE	
531,000	HOCKEY	
436,000	SKATING	
354,000	BASKETBALL	
336,000	GYMNASTICS	
330,000	RUNNING	
277,300	BALLET	
230,000	KARATE	

Canadian children play a lot more than just hockey.

a lot like football. But it is more rough and tumble. The players do not wear much padding.

Canada's vast landscapes and many lakes make it perfect for summer fun. Long ago, Aboriginal Peoples made trails to hunt, fish, and travel. Later explorers and settlers walked across the land. Today people hike for pleasure. Canada has a network of hiking trails throughout the country.

The Trans Canada Trail passes through every province and territory. When complete, it will connect nearly 500 shorter trails. It will stretch almost 24,000 kilometres. People will be able to hike from the Atlantic to the Pacific and on to the Arctic Ocean.

Many Canadians enjoy kayaking and canoeing. Kayaks were first used by Aboriginal Peoples, such as Aleut and Inuit hunters. Many Aboriginal Peoples made open canoes of wood and birch bark.

Canada has beaches by the Atlantic and Pacific Oceans. Canada is also rich in lakes. Many people enjoy swimming, fishing, and playing at lakeshores. Manitoba is called the "Land of 10,000 Lakes." People often have cabins along the lakes.

FAST FACT

People come from all around the world to fish in Canada. Long ago, fish were an important food for Aboriginal Peoples. They caught fish using handmade nets or spears. In winter, they fished through holes in lake ice. Today, many Aboriginal Peoples still fish as part of their way of life. Other Canadians fish for food and for sport.

Chapter Four

ENJOYING NATURE

There are many ways Canadians enjoy the outdoors. They may watch animals in their natural **habitats**. Canada offers many wildlife tours. Guides tell visitors about the animals of Canada, their history, habits, and habitat.

The oceans around Canada have 33 kinds of whales. People often go on whale-watching boat tours from Vancouver and Victoria, British Columbia. They may see orcas and humpbacks. Seals, dolphins, and sea lions may also swim nearby.

Bird watchers do more than just watch. They also listen. Every kind of bird has a different call. Noisy birds

On the Atlantic coast, whale watchers can see humpback, *pictured*, beluga, blue, and sperm whales.

What activities do people in your community like? How do they differ from activities in other provinces and territories?

Hundreds of parks and resorts offer great camping in Canada from coast to coast.

in the Northwest Territories include trumpeter swans and whooping cranes. Snowy owls hoot in Quebec. Banff National Park has nutcrackers and mountain chickadees. Seabirds along the rocky Atlantic coast include puffins, murres, and terns. The official bird of Yukon is the raven.

Camping is popular in Canada. In the West, campers often go to Pacific Rim National Park in British Columbia. In Ontario, Algonquin Provincial Park is a very popular camping spot.

Some people camp in tents. Others take a trailer or RV. They get away from big cities to enjoy nature. Some people may even sleep inside a traditional Aboriginal teepee. They can be found in national parks across the country.

Indoors or outdoors, in summer, fall, winter, or spring, Canada is always a great place to have fun.

GLOSSARY

HABITATS
the natural living areas of an animal or a plant

MULTICULTURAL
several different cultures together in one place

PANNING
looking for gold by scooping gravel from stream beds with a wide, shallow pan

SCULPTING
carving or shaping a piece of art from a material such as snow, wood, or stone

SHOWCASES
features in a positive way

TATTOO
an outdoor military display

TRADITIONS
beliefs or practices handed down through generations, often by word of mouth

TREADS
the parts of a tire that touch the ground

TO LEARN MORE

BOOKS

Aloian, Molly. *Cultural Traditions in Canada*. St. Catharines, ON: Crabtree, 2014.

Hudak, Heather C. *Dance*. Calgary: Weigl, 2010.

McDowell, Pamela. *Ceremonies and Celebrations*. Calgary: Weigl, 2015.

WEBSITES

CANADA TREASURE TREK!
www.tvokids.com/games/canadastreasuretrek

CANADIAN GEOGRAPHIC KIDS!
www.canadiangeographic.ca/kids/default.asp

THE KIDS' SITE OF CANADIAN SETTLEMENT
www.collectionscanada.gc.ca/settlement/kids/index-e.html

INDEX

ABOUT THE AUTHOR

Paula Morrow is a former magazine and book editor. Now a writing coach, she speaks at writers' conferences and presents workshops on writing for children and young adults.